"My mother was told that I was living a lesbian life with Valerie. All she had to say was that I was living a lesbian life, and that was grounds to have you committed to an insane asylum...I was picked up, thrown in a police car, and they took me down into the psycho ward of general hospital."

—Donna Smith

"Well, honey, when I went to [Greenwich Village in the early 1960s], there was lesbians in the streets in droves. Women that looked like men, men that looked like women. Women with their hair slicked back, the femmes with the beehives...I found myself a girlfriend; she was a femme type. And I loved it, I really felt at peace."

—Red Jordan Arobateau

BEFORE STONEWALL:
THE MAKING OF A GAY AND LESBIAN COMMUNITY

The Naiad Press, Inc.
1988

Printed in the United States of America
First Edition

Cover and book design by: John Lewis (New York)

Library of Congress Cataloging in Publication Data

Weiss, Andrea.
    Before Stonewall.

    "An illustrated historical guide to the Emmy Award
winning film."
    Bibliography: p. 80
    1. Gay liberation movement — United States —
History — 20th century. I. Schiller, Greta. II. Title.
HQ76.8.U5W43 1988   306.7'66'0973   88-9111
ISBN 0-941483-20-7

For our friend Bill Daughton,
dedicated, assiduous film editor of *Before Stonewall*,
who died of AIDS in June 1987

in the hope that the fear and ignorance that sanction such
tragedies will soon give way to knowledge and compassion.

ACKNOWLEDGMENTS

Our heartfelt thanks and admiration go to the many women and men who opened up their homes and their lives, by contributing their stories and scrapbooks for inclusion in the film and in this book. They are a constant source of inspiration to us. We also want to thank the many people we worked with in making the film, especially John Scagliotti, Executive Producer; Robbie Rosenberg, Co-Director; Bill Daughton, Editor; Vito Russo, Consultant; Peter J. Friedman, Assistant Editor; as well as the many, many others who put in countless hours of research, fundraising, and other work.

Special appreciation goes to Ann Mari Buitrago, Maureen Brady, Ginny Yans, Keith Hefner, Liz Sher, Bob Freedman, and Melissa Cahill for their comments and suggestions in the last-minute preparation of this book.

This book was funded in part by grants from the New York Council for the Humanities, Resist Foundation, and Chicago Resource Center, through the fiscal sponsorship of the Foundation for the Community of Artists. We are very grateful for their support.

All research and photographs were culled from the files of the Before Stonewall Film Project. We thank the following institutions and individuals for providing the images that appear in these pages:
Jim Wickloff, Jheri Williams, Johnnie Phelps, Harry Otis, Schomberg Center for Black Culture, Kinsey Institute for Sex Research, Hank Vilas, Naiad Press, Lesbian Herstory Archives, Donald Hoffman, Teddie Boutte, Randy Wicker, Ret Coller, Donna Smith, Kay Tobin, Henry van Dieckoff.

Finally, we'd like to thank John Lewis, as well as Barbara Grier and Donna McBride of Naiad Press, for their efforts in publishing this book.

"Becoming Visible" was previously published, in a slightly different form, in the *New York Native*, July 1, 1985.

ABOUT THE AUTHORS

Andrea Weiss won an Emmy Award for her research on "Before Stonewall." She produced and directed, with Greta Schiller, "International Sweethearts of Rhythm: America's Hottest All-Girl Band," which premiered at the 1986 New York Film Festival at Lincoln Center. Her articles and essays have appeared in *Ms.,The Advocate, Cineaste, Conditions*, and other journals. Andrea is currently pursuing a Ph.D. in American women's history at Rutgers University.

Greta Schiller is the Director and Co-Producer of the award-winning film, "Before Stonewall." With Andrea Weiss, she founded the feminist film company, Jezebel Productions, and directed two highly acclaimed companion films, "International Sweethearts of Rhythm" and "Tiny & Ruby: Hell Divin' Women." Greta was recently awarded a Fulbright Arts Fellowship to work in film production in Great Britain.

Contents

Contents

Foreword

by Barbara Grier

Before Stonewall, the movie, gave the world the first complete yet concise view of the community of lesbians and gay men in the United States from 1900 on. **Before Stonewall**, the book, rounds out this picture with the historical documentation of our roots.

Until **Before Stonewall** the world knew little of the existence of our community in earlier years, much less how the life of that community evolved into the modern lesbian and gay movement.

Books and movies like **Before Stonewall** help inculcate in us a sense of pride in our past generations. They provide us with the vital sense of community, without which minority groups cannot hope to overcome social deprivation. Such works are also the tools with which we can reach out to educate the wider community in the battle to achieve social equality.

After thirty-five years of activity in the gay community, I recognize that the goal of full freedom for all gay people will probably not be realized in my lifetime. But I am comforted by the knowledge that **Before Stonewall**, the movie and the book, will be a source of inspiration and strength for future generations to reach this goal.

Introduction

Today in the United States, for the first time in history, there is a visible and vocal lesbian and gay community, and a political movement for gay rights. Although gay people continue to face family rejection and social discrimination, still the existence of this community and political movement provides crucial emotional support and the possibility of organizing to fight back against injustices. Gay communities exist in virtually every American city and town; in the past fifteen or so years this subculture has developed its own newspapers, social clubs, bookstores, political organizations, businesses, restaurants, and even churches and synagogues where gay people can meet each other and find the acceptance often denied them by the larger society.

Virtually none of these visible, organized institutions existed before the Stonewall riot of 1969, an event considered to be the birth of the modern gay liberation movement. What was Stonewall, and why did it happen? Where did this unprecedented movement, with its own culture, community, and economic and political power, come from? These were the driving questions behind the making of the film, "Before Stonewall". To find the answers we had to understand what life was like for the many homosexual men and women who lived before there was a gay movement, who lived before

Stonewall.

On the night of June 27, 1969, hundreds of gay men poured out of the Stonewall Inn in New York City's Greenwich Village, hurling bricks and bottles at the police. No longer willing to put up with police harassment that included the routine arrest of patrons of this and many other gay bars, gay people fought back and sparked three days of rioting in the streets. This explosion of social violence was a watershed event in the lives of millions of American lesbians and gay men. Beginning with Stonewall, an isolated and stigmatized group of individuals transformed themselves into a vital and influential political movement. In the process, our society's view of homosexuality evolved from being a shameful personal problem that no one would talk about, to becoming a controversial social issue, debated on TV talk shows, in newspaper columns, and at dinner tables across America.

Yet the history of lesbians and gay men in the United States has largely remained a hidden history. Our knowledge of gay American experience in this century is negligible, (mis)informed primarily by prejudice and myth. This is true even though the artistic, scientific, political, cultural, intellectual, and economic contributions of gay people to our society have been enormous. And it is true even though gay people have existed and continue to exist in every American village, city or town, among every race, ethnic group, and religion, in each age group and in both genders. The film "Before Stonewall" begins to correct this giant oversight, filling the void left by school textbooks and media programs that cover American history but fail to mention the second largest, perhaps even the single largest, minority group in America.

"Before Stonewall" relies on the stories of "ordinary" people who lived their lives as gay men and women during a time when there was little acceptance or understanding anywhere they turned. The people who speak in the film are obviously recounting their own individual, first-hand experiences, but they were selected for the film because they also represent a much broader population across the country who have had similar experiences. Since the stories of homosexuals are rarely found in history books, this technique of oral history is the primary means we have to learn about and preserve this forgotten heritage.

The oral history interviews are interwoven with archival materials: visual records that document a particular time and place in history. We used old newsreels, clips from Hollywood movies, newspapers, magazines, and television news —

— all of which provided the perspective of the dominant culture on homosexuality. But we also used photographs, scrapbooks, home movies, and personal memorabilia belonging to individual gay men and women, in order to understand the gay subculture's view of itself. Not surprisingly, these two different kinds of sources revealed two different, yet related, histories.

When we have appeared at film screenings of "Before Stonewall" around the country and in Europe, someone in the audience invariably comments on the unconventional use of archival material: The film makes use of imagery that, if taken out of the context we have given it, at times seems to have nothing to do with homosexuality at all. (An example of this would be the scene of women dancing together in military uniforms during World War II.) This impression may be due to the fact that we are so used to not seeing homosexuality; unless people are labeled as such or conform to certain preconceived stereotypes, the assumption of our culture is that people, interactions, and customs are heterosexual. The inclusion of this material is intended to correct the historical invisibility of gay people, by putting forward the possibility of homosexuality, as well as heterosexuality, as part of human behavior and experience in a given era. (Please see "Becoming

Visible: On Doing Research in Lesbian and Gay History," on page 69, about the use of archival footage in the film.)

Another question we have often been asked is why the film begins and ends where it does (and why it doesn't continue up to the present day.) "Before Stonewall" covers the time period from the early 20th century until the Stonewall riots of 1969. We started with 1900 because it was about this time that homosexuality began to be viewed as one aspect of a person's identity, rather than as an isolated sexual act in which anyone might engage. Prior to this, homosexual acts were seen as specific incidents, transgressions or sins, but with the rise of the medical profession by the turn of the century, these acts became identified with the personality of the "transgressor." How this developed is complex and beyond the scope of this book (and the film), but we chose to use the new concept of a homosexual person, rather than simply a homosexual act, as the beginning point for our exploration of the development of the gay movement.

"Before Stonewall" ends with the Stonewall riots because its thesis is, simply put, how the gay subculture developed from isolated individuals into a cohesive force, with sufficient rage and anger to resist police harassment, thereby sparking the Stonewall riots and the mod-

ern gay liberation movement.
"Stonewall" is considered the beginning
of this movement because of its electrify-
ing effect on the political organization of
the gay and lesbian community. For
example, before Stonewall there were
only a handful of gay organizations and
publications; within a year of the
Stonewall rebellion there were hundreds.
Other sources amply document post-
Stonewall events to an extent that gay
people who lived pre-Stonewall could
never have imagined. And so we ended
the film with this transition that signaled
a new era.

Although the film ends nearly a
decade before the advent of AIDS, we feel
a few words are in order, as it has come to
dominate much of the contemporary discourse on gay and lesbian life today. The
AIDS crisis has sparked a new socially
sanctioned anti-homosexual hysteria. An
equally strong movement has risen in the
lesbian and gay community, where institutions have been created that serve as
models for a compassionate, humane
political and social response to a severe
medical epidemic. The rapid development
of the gay and lesbian community and the
continued resilience of gay people since
the Stonewall riot have made this mobi-
lized effort possible.

The history presented in "Before
Stonewall" is not simply one of oppres-

sion and discrimination against people who were perceived as being "different." The interviews reveal how even under such conditions people can exert some control over their lives and their destinies, they can maintain a sense of dignity, and they can fight injustice to effect change. An important part of shaping our own futures is learning about and gaining inspiration from those who have faced similar challenges in the past.

The Twilight World:
The Turn of the Century to the 1930's

In the United States in the decades following the turn of the century, most lesbians and gay men believed that they were the only ones ever to feel an attraction to members of the same sex. As homosexuality was never discussed outside of medical journals and religious prohibitions, there was no way of knowing that others even existed. The idea of living as a lesbian or gay man did not enter the consciousness of most people. Turn of the century America was primarily a rural society, with very little interchange between city and country lifestyles. While small pockets of gay life offered companionship and a wider range of choices in the cities, we know of few such alternatives in the countryside or in small towns, where the majority of the population, homosexual and heterosexual, lived.

This aloneness, this feeling of "what's wrong with me," was prevalent. One woman in "Before Stonewall" says, "I felt like I was the only one, until I left home. Home was in North Carolina." Another recalls, "I was brought up on a farm. I knew enough not to talk about it. I knew enough to hide [my sexuality]."

For both men and women, marriage was an expected way of life. To not marry cast you as an outsider from society. Women in particular had very few alternatives to heterosexual marriage unless they had family money available to them.

Societal mores also kept women within the confines of the private sphere— the home and family. Here opportunities to express any sexuality, outside of procreation, were extremely rare, although some middle-class women did develop intimate love relationships dubbed "Boston Marriages." These relationships were more or less accepted as close friendships because lesbianism was not really believed to be possible, and because women were considered to be more romantic and emotional than men, which would naturally lead on occasion to intimate relations with each other. Throughout history there are incidents of women who broke from the traditions of society to live as they chose, but such cases are the rare exception — most had few alternatives but to live within a very narrow sphere of life that was designated for women.

Homosexual men, by virtue of the fact that they were men, were allowed greater mobility: greater access to parks, cafes, bars, clubs, and other meeting places. In the private sphere they were also allowed greater freedom to act on sexual desires. So although it is likely that

they often felt guilt about their homosexual attractions, still there were places
available for them to meet other men with
similar inclinations. Harry Hay, a vision-
ary man involved with the theatre and
with political activism, describes how
such a liaison might happen:

> *Sometimes you would look into a*
> *person's eyes, he would look into*
> *your eyes, and all of a sudden you*
> *would know through the eyes. Or you*
> *knew each other by a red necktie. It*
> *was very daring to wear a hanky*
> *that matched the tie and the moment*
> *you saw that, no matter what the*
> *color was, you figured that there was*
> *a brother there. After you had*
> *cruised each other back and forth by*
> *looking in the same window at the*
> *same time for quite a while, you*
> *might ask a person, "Do you have a*
> *match?" or "Can you tell me the*
> *time?" These were the little things*
> *that we would be using in the twen-*
> *ties, and we were still using in the*
> *thirties, I might add.*

Men could more easily live a double
life — as a straight, family man, but with
an illicit sexual life. For some men, this
double life was not possible; they were
simply unable to bend their desires to fit
the heterosexual role of husband and

father. These homosexuals, by not pretending to be heterosexual, possibly had less internal conflict raging within them, but on the other hand were treated as outcasts. Relegated to the outer fringes of society, they often became part of the disreputable world described by Harry Hay:

That whole society would have been known as the gay society, or the gay world, or the world of the demi-monde, the world of twilight, the world of night. And so all the people who had to deal with that area were always considered totally disrespectable. And therefore of very questionable morals. This would be the world of dance, this was the world of the artist, this was the world of the people who flitted around the parks and forests at night...The people who would be out at night wandering around loose without going specifically from one place to another were obviously there for no good purpose. And this is known as the world of the demi-monde, this is the twilight world as it was known in the earliest 20th century, and it is the world of the gay people.

While homosexual men and women lived on the fringes of society, developing their own set of customs and values, they of course were influenced by and lived economically within the dominant society. To live as, or be seen with, known homosexuals was a risky venture. To be found out could (and often did) result in imprisonment; loss of job, family and friends; commitment to an institution; and possibly even suicide. Donna Smith, a retired bookkeeper, speaks in "Before Stonewall" of her experience in the 1930s:

> *My mother was told that I was living a lesbian life with Valerie. All she had to say was that I was living a lesbian life and that was grounds to have you committed to an insane asylum... I was picked up off the streets, thrown in a police car, and [they] put me down into the psycho ward of the general hospital.*

Because of these very harsh penalties, many people hid their feelings, not only from family and friends, but also from themselves. The view that homosexuality was unnatural, unhealthy, and a dangerous moral threat to society was often internalized by gays themselves. Everywhere they turned they were told their feelings were wrong. Such self-denial and self-hatred must have led to much unhappiness, bitterness and frustration. Some gays were able to find the inner resources to overcome these nega-

Old Maids?

tive messages; often they lived in couples, under the protective cover of "old maids," "sisters," "brothers," "cousins," etc. It is particularly difficult to research and uncover the history of homosexual life in America — because so much of it was deeply concealed from and invisible to the dominant culture.

* * *

Although most homosexuals in America continued to live in isolation, fear, self-denial and secrecy, with the onset of the Roaring 20s alternatives to the small-town lifestyle began to emerge in the rapidly expanding cities. The Twenties witnessed a large migration from rural areas to the cities, lured by economic prosperity, a sense of adventure, and new opportunities. An enticing sense of hope and optimism swept across the country. Soldiers who had been overseas during World War I brought new ideas back to the States. The then-popular song, "How you gonna keep 'em down on the farm after they've seen Paree," accurately reflects this phenomenon. The lesbian and gay life provided colorful and prominent features in European cities such as Paris, Berlin, and London; for those homosexuals who were introduced to this subculture while stationed overseas during the war, the possibility of a different life was posed for the first time.

A variety of new ethnic cultures was brought to America by the massive influx of European immigrants in the early 20th century. The foreign languages, dress, and customs they brought with them changed the nature of American cities and introduced many new models of behavior, both from their countries of origin and in the amalgam of old and new.

"New Women" put off marriage, wore relatively unrestricted clothing, and had an attitude of social defiance.

These social and economic changes, combined with the anonymity that sheer numbers afforded, contributed to the breakdown of rigid social norms designed to ensure conformity to one set of values. Although many conservative forces continued to prevail, there also existed in certain areas of the cities a greater tolerance toward anything different.

The passage of the hard-won right to suffrage, and the carefree attitude that the end of the War signaled, both contributed to the phenomenon of the "New Woman" — who put off marriage to live on her own, wore relatively unrestricted clothing, and had an attitude of social defiance and sexual liberation. Flappers wore short skirts, bobbed their hair, and danced the Charleston throughout American cities. The "New Woman" image reflected unprecedented social freedom for women; however, for many it came to a quick end when they realized they were pregnant or simply flat broke. But its existence contributed to the realization by many women that they could live life more fully than simply as wife and mother. For lesbians, this realization was crucial.

As Prohibition was the law of the land, adventurous gay men and women gathered at popular speakeasies — unadvertised social clubs where illegal alcoholic drinks were served — in bohemian neighborhoods such as San Francisco's Barbary Coast, New Orlean's French Quarter, and New York City's Harlem and Greenwich Village. The social life of the speakeasies was a major part of the Roaring Twenties. Harry Otis, a dancer and writer, remembers that decade with fondness:

The main thought behind [the Roaring Twenties] was to break the law and live as wildly as you could. And everybody did, because speakeasies were all over town, even the old residences had speakeasies in the basement. Now a lot of people write about prohibition, but they

THE GREENWICH VILLAGE BALL

15th Annual Edition

Friday, Jan. 15th
Webster Hall
119 East 11th St.
10 P. M. 'til dawn

Come all ye Revelers!—Dance the night unto dawn—come when you like, with whom you like—wear what you like—

Unconventional? Oh, to be sure—only do be discreet!

Tickets $2.00 in advance or $3.00 at the door
Boxes $15.00

Cynthia White, 11 Fifth Ave.   STuy. 9-4674

CONTINUOUS MUSIC
MIDNIGHT DIVERTISSEMENTS

21

don't bring out the fact that every-body was breaking the law because it was the thing to do.

Harry Otis, circa 1925

In these urban communities a "homo-sexual underground" flourished. Books, plays and music with gay themes were brought out by major publishers and pro-ducers. Barbara Grier, author of *The Lesbian in Literature: A Bibliography* and a long-time lesbian publisher, says:

There were so many lesbian novels in the United States [before] 1940...There were more than 500 novels with clearly discernible lesbian content published.

Many social, political, and economic forces converge to create change. Publication of books can influence millions of people, directly or peripherally. Radclyffe Hall, an aristocratic English lesbian, wrote one such novel, *The Well of Loneliness*. Its publication in America in 1928 caused great upheavals in the American judicial system, spilling out into the newspapers and becoming a topic of conversation for people across America. Although the novel ends tragically for the lesbian lovers, its sympathy for the two women, its open disdain for homophobia, and its author's first hand knowledge of the gay subculture were enough for one judge to call the book's moral stance "worse than throwing acid in a young person's eyes."

For gay people, this was often the first time they'd heard any public discourse on the topic of homosexuality. Especially for those not fortunate enough to have found the pockets of gay urban subculture, the book took on magnified importance. It was a bestseller, a must on any with-it coffee table. Mabel Hampton, an avid collector of lesbian novels, says,

*Well, you know how it all started: **The Well of Loneliness**. From then on, anything that came past, I read it.*

THE WELL OF LONELINESS

"Worse than throwing acid in a young person's eyes."

Mabel was part of another marginal community as well— the cultural resurgence of American Blacks known as the Harlem Renaissance. Centered in the Harlem neighborhood of New York, this prolific wave of Black poets, musicians, artists, dancers, photographers, and singers, as well as of Black-owned businesses, included many gay men and lesbians. While Blacks were prohibited by law and custom from entering white establishments across the country, whites on the other hand were welcome in Black clubs, which were much more accepting of difference— racial or sexual. It is hard to imagine today, but the Harlem clubs most remembered by history were the ones that catered exclusively to white audiences while featuring Black entertainers. While these tourists were catching a glimpse of the Harlem Renaissance in white-only clubs, the more adventurous gays, Blacks and whites, were part of a free-wheeling, wide open tolerance. Richard Bruce Nugent, an artist of the Harlem Renaissance, describes the Black nightlife like this:

Langston Hughes

You see, those places were not gay but they were open. The whole atmosphere was open. It was almost impossible not to know everybody that happened to pass through Harlem at that time. Black, white, grizzle or gray, it doesn't make any difference.

These pockets of bohemian subculture that sprung up in major American cities during the 1920s provided a relatively comfortable environment in which many gay men and women, cast out of genteel society, could create. Many of America's important writers, artists and thinkers emerged from the homosexual underground, including Romaine Brooks, Langston Hughes, Margaret Anderson, Tennessee Williams, and Gertrude Stein.

The publication of Radclyffe Hall's novel, *The Well of Loneliness*, the success of the lesbian-themed hit Broadway play, "The Captive," and the production of Oscar Wilde's "Salome" into a film with an all-gay cast attest to the loosening of social and sexual mores in the Roaring Twenties. But the times they were a'changing: the relative economic prosperity came to a halt in 1929, and the hard times of the Great Depression led to increased racial and sexual discrimination, and political and social unrest. The censorship forces which had been fighting a losing battle throughout the 1920s and early '30s eventually prevailed, and by 1935 the motion picture code banned all references to homosexuality. In Germany, the Nazis had come to power and many who were thought to be homosexual were put in concentration camps with Jews and other "undesirables." In America, the attitude of tolerance that characterized the 1920s gave way to a less generous atmosphere focused almost exclusively on survival and self-preservation. For gay people in the 1930s, the closet door that had opened a crack in the previous decade was closing once more, but for those who had made the transition from rural and small town life to a more anonymous lifestyle in the city, a certain freedom remained.

Ted Rolfs, a retired Merchant Marine, came to New York as a young man in 1932, from his home state of Wisconsin. What he found was the companionship of others like himself, where he could lead an active gay life within the perimeters of New York débutante balls and political circles. He even met Dr. Magnus Hirschfield, the most famous sexologist and fighter for gay rights in the world. A German refugee, whose prestigious, controversial Institute for Sexual Science was burned by the Nazis, Hirschfield sought to continue his campaign for tolerance and acceptance for homosexuals. Only 50 years ago, the most liberal, scientifically progressive thought on homosexuality considered gays as members of a "Third Sex." As usual, the individuals who were living these "deviant" lifestyles were far ahead of the social scientists, psychologists, lawyers and clergy whose task it was to study and analyze homosexuality. As mentioned previously, many gay people were prominent citizens, contributing to the arts, sciences, politics, and culture of the society they lived in, but they were for the most part invisible to the analytical eyes of these professionals.

The underground community Ted Rolfs discovered was subtle, and one needed to be quite cautious— but it lay simmering beneath the surface, erupting in major cities around the Western world with the outbreak of World War II.

Hank Vilas, one of the thousands of homosexuals who responded to the call to serve his country during World War II.

The 1940s:

The War Years & the Post-War Years

When the United States finally entered World War II in 1941, the social fabric of this country changed radically and substantially in ways that today are still not fully understood. Government and industry needed able-bodied workers to support the full scale military and homefront battles. The very definition of "able bodied" was transformed from white men to embrace women and men of all races and colors, as well as sexual persuasions. Chuck Rowlands, coming of age in St. Paul, recalls his surprise at the number of gay officers in the Army:

> *My first assignment in the Army was in the induction station in Fort Snelling, which instantly became called the "seduction station." I found that all the people I had known in the gay bars in Minneapolis and St. Paul were officers who were running this seduction station. When recruits would be lined up by the thousands, as they would be each morning outside our windows, all of us would rush to the windows and look out and express great sorrow that all these beautiful boys were going to be killed or maimed or something in the war.*

The contradictions inherent in any society are magnified during war time.

While Japanese-Americans were targeted as scapegoats— their homes and businesses were seized, and entire families were held in California internment camps for the war's duration— Blacks were crucial to the mobilization effort. The abundance of war jobs in the cities meant full employment for Blacks as well as whites, for women as well as men. Middle class women previously confined to the home or to acceptable "female" professions now could travel unescorted by men, enter traditionally male jobs — from scientist to jazz musician to shipbuilder — receive respectable pay and often have day care centers look after their children. These changes had tremendous impact on all Americans. For lesbians it was particularly important that women were given opportunity to make a living wage. This meant that they could live independently of a male income, previously essential for even minimum economic comfort. Prior to the war effort and the resulting dramatic changes, women were relegated to the private sphere of the church, family and home. This was now breaking down as it became acceptable for women to travel, to work alone, and to congregate with other women in public places.

Lisa Ben, whose name is a pseudonym (and an anagram for "Lesbian"), moved to Los Angeles seeking secretarial work and immediately rented her own apartment. She recalls her first encounters with lesbians: the women of her apartment building were sunning themselves, talking about Sue and Sally and Mary—but no Bob, Bill or John. One of the women asked her whether she was gay, and in her naivete she replied, "I suppose so, at least I'm happy." This was enough for her to be invited to a lesbian bar, where she "felt at home for the first time in my life."

The war years were characterized by living environments that were temporary and sex segregated. Hotels and dormitories catering to working women, such as Lisa Ben, sprang up in the cities. In these female settings, away from families, friends and small-town mentality, many lesbians discovered their sexual preferences. Although, obviously, all women didn't have lesbian relations, and among those who did, not all remained homosexual, many lesbians found places of comfort and solace, taking female lovers for the first time. Protected by the numbers of single women in civilian life, they were able to co-exist with straight society in places normally forbidden to them. The places previously somewhat accessible, such as bars, grew in popularity.

In the 1940s, the U.S. military recruited thousands of women into its ranks. In unprecedented numbers, women signed up, eager to be useful to

the war effort. The single minded focus on the war meant, for the most part, greater social acceptance of everyone— homosexuals included— who could be useful in working for victory. Sergeant Johnnie Phelps, a woman who joined the military because "when December 7th came, everybody was expected to do something..." found that

> there was a tolerance for lesbianism if they needed you. If you had a job to do that was a specialist kind of job or if you were in a theatre of operations where bodies were needed, then they tolerated anything, just about.

Sergeant Phelps had the opportunity to test this tolerance on one occasion when General Eisenhower, her commanding officer, asked her to ferret out the lesbians in her WAC battalion. She replied:

Sir, I'll be happy to do this investiga-
tion for you but you'll have to know
that the first name on the list will be
mine... I think the General should be
aware that among those women are
the most highly decorated women in
the war. There have been no cases of
illegal pregnancies, there have been
no cases of AWOL, there have been
no cases of misconduct, and as a
matter of fact, every six months the
General has awarded us a commen-
dation for meritorious service.

Eisenhower, knowing better than to look a gift horse in the mouth, simply said, "Forget the order."

The military personnel that flooded the port cities during the war included large numbers of gay men who congregated in the emerging social institution of the gay underground— the gay bar. Jim Kepner, a man who "came out" in the midst of these radical social changes, describes it like this:

Certainly [the war] brought a lot
more people from the hinterlands
out into conditions where they
weren't living in small towns, where
they were freer, where they met
other people and, male and female,
got into close, same-sex close rela-

tions and developed friendships. On the nights out, groups of soldiers may go looking for women and end up finding one another.

George Buse, who joined the Marines to prove his manhood and disprove the stereotype that all gay men are effeminate, explains how the war years changed the way in which gay people viewed themselves:

The effect of World War II is really, truly profound. Our country will never again be what it was before that war. Gay people began to recognize that there were other people like themselves from other parts of the country. Even though we were totally "closeted" then, at least there was a certain perception that we weren't geographically isolated.

After the war, many gay men and women remained in the large, anonymous cities. Here they distanced themselves from the scrutiny of their families back home and found companionship in America's growing urban gay population. There was a great push to return society to its previous set of social norms: male veterans reclaimed their jobs; women were forced out of the workplace and back into the kitchen. But too many changes had already taken place that could not be undone. Lesbians and the many other women for whom the kitchen was not an option lost the economic gains they had made during the war. (And even the kitchen had changed, to minimize the amount of time working women had to spend there.) Black soldiers who had fought to defend "democracy" abroad came back to experience second class citizenship at home, and the beginning of civil rights activity in the U.S. was sparked. The poet Allen Ginsberg makes it clear why for homosexuals a return to the previous existence of secrecy and fear was also not possible:

In the Forties the Bomb dropped. In the Forties the entire planet was threatened biologically. In the Forties there was a recovery from a total breakdown of all morality in the concentration camps. For those of us who were homosexual, it was the realization of, why are we being intimidated by a bunch of jerks who don't know anything about life? Who were they to tell us what to feel and how we're supposed to behave?

The Kinsey Report, first published in 1948, also changed the way in which homosexuality was viewed by society and by gay people themselves. Dr. Evelyn

Hooker, a psychologist credited with doing groundbreaking research on homosexuality, indicates the extent to which Kinsey's study had an effect:

Homosexuality was thought to be a comparatively rare phenomenon, until Kinsey came along and provided very good evidence that actually there were of course roughly twenty million gay men and women. That was important because it gave great hope to gay people and lesbians, because they realized that they were not a tiny minority but actually a very sizeable proportion of the population.

By the late 1940s, however, a conservative tide swept across the country. The House UnAmerican Activities Committee (HUAC) attack on Communists also implicated gay people and anyone who seemed to be "different." George Buse recalls,

People were looking for enemies of all sorts everywhere: perverts, queers, anything, anybody who's deviant. People who were dissidents of any kind, sexually, socially, politically, what have you. And they were looking for people like this under every bed, around every corner and behind every door. It was a whole different spirit.

Gay men and lesbians did not stop
being homosexual; they simply adapted as
best they could to the changing times.
This growing atmosphere of fear and conformity caught hold and would remain
throughout, in fact would become charac-
teristic of, the entire next decade.

Harry Hay: an interview

Harry Hay has devoted his long, productive life to the pursuit of justice. As a young man, he was a member of the Industrial Workers of the World (IWW); in the 30's in Los Angeles, he worked with a radical theatre troupe, performing agitprop with members of the Communist Party. Here we focus on his experiences in the midst of the Cold War, as founder of America's first homophile rights organization, the Mattachine Society, and his continued political activism through the Sixties.

[In] all of the activities that I got involved in during the 1930's and 40's, I had the naive assumption that I would work against [another group's] oppression for this period, and then when I got an idea of how gay people could organize, that they would help us because we had helped them, quid pro quo. It was during the second World War that I realized this wasn't going to happen... In 1948, I went to a gay party and we started talking about forming a "Bachelors for Wallace" [for President]... We would have a plank and educate people about who we were, about how we weren't bad people; we would end entrapment, and begin a whole new movement for the gay peoples. I was so excited, I went home and wrote it all up. When I called them the next day, they all said "forget it honey;" it was the [influence of] the beer.

By this time, the Jews couldn't be the next scapegoat, and Blacks had formed the National Negro Congress to protect themselves, and we in the [Communist] Party were discussing the rise of fascism in America; we were all afraid of what was to happen here. I felt we [homosexuals] would be the next victims. The fact is that the government was already pointing to homosexuals in government as Communist threats, saying that they were being used as spies by the Soviet Union because they were being blackmailed. I wasn't thinking in terms of gay rights yet; that was much later. My thinking was that what we have to do right now is to find out who we are, where we've been, what kind of contribution can be made [to society at large], and what are we for? For the next two years, I searched for people to join me [to start the organization, the Mattachine Society]. Ultimately there were five of us, and then seven, in the original group. We were all terrified of the police, so we made all decisions by unanimous consent, and kept the leadership small. We thought if we all positively agreed on it, we couldn't make a mistake. One of our first ideas was to hold discussion groups; we would sit around and talk about being gay, and within a very short time, we had a whole series of discussion groups going. We had an initiation ceremony -- we'd all hold hands and we had ritualistic things that we said, something like, "No gay person coming into the world will ever again have to feel alone and unwanted and rejected."

To the straight public, the word homosexual meant willful, perverse, defiant, sick young heterosexuals who are performing unnatural and therefore criminal acts. So we realized in order to get them to see us as people, we had to break through this madness. There was this total conspiracy of silence, and we knew that if we ever broke through and got into the newspapers, we had to call ourselves something they didn't know, so they 'd have to ask us. I spent hours going through the Greek lexicon and found the word homophile, which

Harry Hay, founder of the Mattachine Society, on location at the International Gay and Lesbian Archives with director Greta Schiller.

means lover of same. Our very first public victory was winning the case of entrapment against Dale Jennings. We thought this was really significant, so we sent information out to all the newspapers. But not one paper or radio station covered it. Total silence. Not even the leftist papers covered it.

The magazine [Mattachine Review] was started in 1951, and our first Constitutional Convention was held in 1953. By then the organization was growing by leaps and bounds, and we needed some kind of organization to contain it. We drew up a constitution, and so did the people from San Francisco -- all these conservative guys who had voted for Nixon and Eisenhower -- and they were worried about all these accusations that the leadership was leftist. We realized we were losing. We felt very strongly that the organization had to stay liberal, those were our roots. That is when we resigned from the organization, and [the more conservative members] took over.

* * *

The first national homophile conference was in Kansas City in 1965. By this time the east coast people are very concerned with the image of the homosexual... But here on the west coast, we had passed a resolution that began, "Whereas the homosexual has no image to lose...," which was totally rejected on the east coast. Our feeling was that we weren't interested in respectability, we were interested in self respect, a very different thing. John [Burnside, his long-time lover/partner] and I were involved in the anti-war movement by now, and the counterculture.

Along Telegraph Avenue in Berkeley there were open political forums, and we would go up there and be part of the counterculture and anti-war movements... One night a young woman started asking John and me about our lives together. We told her about ourselves, about the gay movement, about how we were involved in the peace movement as gay men, and all of a sudden we're talking to 100 to 150 people sitting around us. They're all saying, "hey, we've never heard anyone talk about gay lifestyles as a positive lifestyle. We hope you guys come back and keep talking about this."

Articles about the gay lifestyle began to appear in the underground press here. We began to challenge them openly, [arguing that] if they were going to get rid of the prejudices their parents had, they should get rid of their prejudices vis-a-vis homosexuals as well... When Stonewall began a new movement here, one of the first big activities was a "Gay In" in 1970. You see what was happening here, what's really important, is that we were laying a powder train. And when Stonewall comes, all of a sudden that powder train takes off.

FEDERAL VIGILANCE ON PERVERTS ASKED

Senate Group Says They Must Be Kept Out of Government Because of Security Risk

WASHINGTON, Dec. 15 (AP)—A Senate investigating group labeled sexual perverts today as dangerous security risks and demanded strict and careful screening to keep them off the Government payroll. It said that many Federal agencies had not taken "adequate steps to get these people out of Government."

Filing a report to the Senate after a six-month investigation by an Expenditures subcommittee, the chairman, Senator Clyde R. Hoey, Democrat of North Carolina, declared:

"If Government agencies will investigate properly each complaint of sex perversion and thereafter follow the present adequate Civil Service rules, these perverts can be put out of Government and kept out."

Many perverts have been employed, Mr. Hoey said, and he pledged that his subcommittee would keep a close check on the situation.

Stressing the risk that the Government takes in employing a sex deviate or keeping one on the payroll, the subcommittee said:

"The lack of emotional stability which is found in most sex perverts, and the weakness of their moral fiber, makes them susceptible to the blandishments of foreign espionage agents."

Called 'Prey to Blackmailers'

The report also noted that perverts were "easy prey to the blackmailer." It said that Communist and Nazi agents had sought to get secret Government data from Federal employes "by threatening to expose their abnormal sex activities."

The subcommittee criticized the State Department particularly for "mishandling" ninety-one cases of homosexualism among its employes. It said that many of the employes were allowed to resign "for personal reasons," and that no steps were taken to bar them from other Government jobs.

The Senate authorized the investigation last June after an Appropriations subcommittee had estimated there were about 3,750 homosexuals on the Federal payroll in Washington alone. In addition, Senator Joseph H. McCarthy, Republican of Wisconsin, had charged that sexual perverts were employed in the State Department, where they were especially dangerous security risks.

The full-scale investigation was assigned to an Expenditures subcommittee including Senators Hoey, Herbert R. O'Conor of Maryland, James O. Eastland of Mississippi, John L. McClellan of Arkansas, Democrats, and Karl E. Mundt of South Dakota, Margaret Chase Smith of Maine and Andrew Schoeppel of Kansas, Republicans. All of them signed today's report.

---

107 U. S. AIDES OUSTED ON MORALS, SECURITY

WASHINGTON, July 2 (AP)—A House of Representatives committee learned today that 107 State Department employes had been discharged this year as a result of investigations concerning homosexuality or questionable security.

The information came from Scott McLeod, State Department security officer, in a letter to the Government Operations Committee. It was made public by Representative Charles B. Brownson, Republican of Indiana.

Mr. McLeod also said that the department did not have any records identifying the fifty-seven persons who were referred to by Senator Joseph R. McCarthy, Republican of Wisconsin, as Communists in a February, 1950, speech. He said a search of all files had "failed to disclose such a list."

"I might point out that Senator McCarthy did not identify the individuals except by number in his speech," Mr. McLeod added.

Mr. McLeod told the committee he was "reluctant" to give "a categorical answer" to the question: "Are there any Communists now employed in the State Department?"

"I must always presume," he wrote, "that the Soviets are attempting to penetrate an agency as sensitive as the State Department, and * * * I may never conclude that their efforts have been unsuccessful.

"I believe that it goes without saying that no Communists, known to the security officer as such, are on the rolls of the department at this time."

Of the 107 dismissals this year, seventy-four followed investigations of homosexuality, Mr. McLeod said, and thirty-three involved some security question. His gave this breakdown: Dismissals for homosexuality—fifty-four in 1950, 119 in 1951 and 134 in 1952; dismissals for security reasons—twelve in 1950, thirty-five in 1951 and seventy in 1952.

---

126 PERVERTS DISCHARGED

State Department Reports Total Ousted Since Jan. 1, 1951

WASHINGTON, March 25 (UP)—The State Department has discharged 126 homosexuals since Jan. 5, 1951, and is determined to remove any others from the department.

Carlisle H. Humelsine, Deputy Under Secretary for Administration, made the report for the department during recent testimony before a House Appropriations subcommittee.

"There is no doubt in our minds that homosexuals are security risks," and "we have resolved that we are going to clean them up," Mr. Humelsine said in the testimony released today.

"I hope that next year will show that we have broken * * * this particular problem," Mr. Humelsine commented.

PERVERTS CALLED GOVERNMENT PERIL

Gabrielson, G.O.P. Chief, Says They Are as Dangerous as Reds—Truman's Trip Hit

Special to The New York Times

WASHINGTON, April 18—Guy George Gabrielson, Republican National Chairman, asserted today that "sexual perverts who have infiltrated our Government in recent years" were "perhaps as dangerous as the actual Communists."

He elevated what he called the "homosexual angle" to the national political level in his first news letter of 1950, addressed to about 7,000 party workers, under the heading: "This Is the News from Washington."

Giving National Committee support to the campaign of Senator Joseph R. McCarthy, Republican of Wisconsin, against the State Department, but without mentioning him by name, Mr. Gabrielson said:

"As Americans, it is difficult for us to believe that a National Administration would go to such length to cover up and protect subversives, traitors, working against their country in high Government. But it is happening. If there is but one more (Alger) Hiss or (Judith) Coplon still in a key spot, he should be ferreted out. It's no red herring.

"Perhaps as dangerous as the actual Communists are the sexual perverts who have infiltrated our Government in recent years. The State Department has confessed that it has had to fire ninety-one of these. It is the talk of Washington and of the Washington correspondents corps.

"The country would be more aroused over this tragic angle of the situation if it were not for the difficulties of the newspapers and radio commentators in adequately presenting the facts, while respecting the decency of their American audiences."

Mr. Gabrielson's letter, appearing over his signature and made available to reporters, did not expand on his assertion that "sexual perverts" were "perhaps" as dangerous as Communists in Government. He was out of the city today and could not be reached for elaboration.

The chairman's letter also attacked President Truman for labelling his trip to the West Coast next month as "non-political," saying that this was "simply a device to carry on politics at the expense of the taxpayers" and "is 'Pendergastism'" at its worst."

"We must insure in every way at our command that the people understand the nature of this trip; time, spent one month in Florida preparing for another junket away from his White House duties while Congress wallows leaderless," he asserted.

The Dark Fifties:

Although nostalgically remembered by
Hollywood as a time of soda-shops, boy-
meets-girl romances, and pink cadillacs,
for lesbians and gay men the Fifties was
an oppressive, fearful time. McCarthyism
ushered in the new decade: not only
Communists (or those suspected to be)
but also homosexuals, unmarried women
and other non-conformists became victims of a veritable witchhunt conducted
by Senator McCarthy in one branch of
Congress and by the House UnAmerican
Activities Committee in the other.

In a carefully orchestrated campaign
to direct the political, social and economic life of Americans into a conservative,
homogeneous, anti-Soviet force, our
country's leaders criticized McCarthy's
extremist tactics while supporting his dev-
astating campaign. In this period of
American history, known as the Cold War
era, homosexuals were deemed to be
security risks and unstable personalities,
and were systematically investigated and
fired from their jobs.

Because homosexuals for the most
part were full of fear and internalized
self-hatred, the idea of fighting back
against this repression was practically
impossible. One man, Dr. Frank Kameny,
a government scientist at the beginning of
his short career, was called into his superior's office, and told:

We have reason to believe that you are a homosexual. Do you have any comment?" And I said, "What's the information?" And they said, "We can't tell you, that might reveal our sources."...By the end of the year, sort of as a Christmas present, I was out.

In the military, where homosexuals were relatively tolerated during WWII, the tone had changed to one of rigid intolerance. One woman, whose interview in the film is shown only in silhouette — a reminder of the precariousness of today's "gay liberation" — tells of her painful experiences when the military launched an investigation of her. She had joined for the very reasons they advertised — to meet new people, to travel and learn a skill, to escape the confines of her small hometown. For the first time in her life, she felt good about herself and about her contributions to her country. But this feeling would be short lived.

I was in the service during the McCarthy era, '51, 2, and 3. The OSI started an investigation of me because some of the women I had been associated with were under investigation for homosexuality. There was no time of the day when they wouldn't come and get me. I'm

UNDESIRABLE DISCHARGE

FROM THE **ARMED FORCES** OF THE

UNITED STATES OF AMERICA

THIS IS TO CERTIFY THAT

AA B 500 C03 AIRMAN SECOND CLASS REGULAR AIR FORCE

WAS DISCHARGED FROM THE

UNITED STATES AIR FORCE

ON THE 15TH **DAY OF** DECEMBER 1953

AS UNDESIRABLE

J. F RAND
LT COL USAF

DD 1 NOV 51 FORM **258 AF** PREVIOUS EDITIONS OF THIS FORM MAY BE USED 16—80680-8 U. S. GOVERNMENT PRINTING OFFICE

*not easily intimidated but I was total-
ly intimidated by these men. This had
been going on for 10 or 11 months,
and I knew I was at an emotional, a
physical, and a mental breaking
point. I knew it was either tell them
and get out now, or see myself in
some hospital someplace.*

**"Undesirable" only
meant one thing:
homosexuality. A
dishonorable dis-
charge was given for
other violations of
military law.**

   Homosexuals were no more welcome
in social circles than they were in the
work force. Parents tried to have their
children "cured," or failing that,

"disowned" them. Marge Summit, a bar owner in Chicago, remembers the pain of such experiences:

When we were growing up, most of our parents, when they found out we were gay, we were excommunicated from the family, or we were just totally dropped. We weren't invited to a lot of family affairs. My mother tore up my brother's wedding invitation to me because she didn't want the "queer" coming to the wedding. There were a lot of things like that happening to gay kids growing up in the Fifties...

Everything in American culture was geared toward "compulsive heterosexuality"; marriage, two children, a wife in the kitchen of a suburban ranch house were the crucial components of the American Dream. Many lesbians and gay men succumbed to this social pressure and entered marriages for the sake of social acceptance. Barbara Grier explains:

One of the reasons gay people marry is because there is a certain amount of social pressure to do that. Now this social pressure was a lot stronger 20 or 30 years ago than it is now... You either married, or you were a charity case in your own family,

46

because there were very few things you could do [to earn a living]; this was for women.

In the early 1950's, at the crest of this wave of political repression and social conformity, two organizations of self-defined homosexuals were founded on the West Coast — One, Inc. and the Mattachine Society. In an effort to thwart pre-conceived notions that gay people were only interested in sex, the Mattachine Society called itself a homo*phile* organization.

The idea for this secret, cell-like organization originated with an ex-member of the Communist Party, USA. An elaborate system of membership and leadership was proposed by Harry Hay and his fellow travelers.

We didn't know at that point that there had ever been a gay organization of any sort anywhere in the world before. Absolutely no knowledge of that at all. So [we] felt that we had to be very, very careful in everything that we did, and think about it very carefully, or we could make a mistake. If we made a mistake, and got into the papers the wrong way, we could hurt the idea of a movement for years to come. And we were terrified of doing that.

How Can I Ever Face the World?

An early Mattachine Society publication

47

Over the decade, Mattachine's activities grew to include fighting police entrapment and sponsoring discussion groups. The Mattachine Society and One, Inc. published America's first openly homosexual magazines, *The Mattachine Review* and *One*. While these activities sound tame by today's standards, in the 1950's simply to congregate as a group of gay people was a defiant act of courage. At this time, same-sex dancing was illegal, references to homosexuals in movies were illegal, and gay bars were routinely raided by the police.

Most of all, the Mattachine Society helped gay men to come to terms with their homosexuality. For George Buse,

> *It was my first opportunity to meet other gay men in a social setting. And to exchange with each other the pain and agony that we've known. And we helped each other come to the realization that we're not bad people, we're good people.*

The few women who found their way to the Mattachine Society discovered it wasn't the most supportive place for lesbians, and instead turned to yet a third organization to emerge in the Dark Fifties, the Daughters of Bilitis. Founded in 1955 by a lesbian couple in San

Francisco, Del Martin and Phyllis Lyon, its primary goals were to educate lesbians and the general public about lesbianism, and to provide a social gathering place outside of the bars. Barbara Gittings, an early gay activist and member of DOB, recalls that its publication, *The Ladder*,

> *somehow got passed around from hand to hand and they got mailed from one subscriber to another in some other part of the country...and the organization's little office would have letters and phone calls from isolated gay people, sometimes even too afraid to give a name on the telephone, who would say things like"I'm just grateful for your existence, for the sheer existence of groups of my own kind that I can turn to."*

Although gay bars were vulnerable to police attacks and their patrons to alcoholism, it was primarily the bar culture that provided some sense of belonging for America's social outcasts. Police arrests of gay people were frequent — from entrapment to bar raids to any excuse available if they knew someone was gay. After a gay bar raid, local papers would print the names of bar patrons, which often resulted in people losing their jobs. Random violence directed at gay people was not uncommon, but increasingly, nei-

Donald Hoffman (left) and Teddie Boutte (right). "We formed the Lee girls to protect ourselves. I can't remember if it was from Lorelei Lee or General Robert E. Lee, maybe both."

ther was fighting back. According to Teddie Boutte, a drag queen from Louisiana,

We got together because we weren't going to put up with being pushed around. And if somebody pushed one of us around, we would get them.

Women often assumed the complementary roles of butch/femme, in which one woman was more assertive and independent, transgressing the traditional feminine role while the other in many

ways conformed to it. Unlike the dominant culture with its numerous customs and rules for proper, acceptable social behavior, the lesbian world was one with few signposts for social interaction; as such, butch/femme was important in providing a structure for relationships. According to poet and gay cultural theorist Judy Grahn, this structure had deep roots in the gay subculture and manifested behavior that was not so much an imitation of heterosexual roles as it was an exploration of different ways of being female. But in some instances, this "role-playing" was pushed further, so that the "butch" — who appeared to be what our culture defines as "masculine," for safety or other reasons actually passed as a man. Marge Summit explains,

If you wanted to go take a girl out to a real nice intimate dinner, or go into a straight club to see a show but go in as dates, or go to a drive-in, it always worked much better if one looked more like the man and could pass as a man. And chances are you wouldn't find a carload of straight guys pulling up next to you and saying, "Queer, Queer," and then beating the shit out of you. If you looked like a man and tried to pass as a man, you were safer.

A gay wedding in the
mid-Fifties.

In the Fifties, homosexual men
exhibited a great range of self-expression,
from the most masculine men, who passed
as straight, to the more flamboyant drag
queens who lived on the fringes of society.
But for all gay men, "camping it up," the
self-conscious parody of heterosexual
behavior and attitudes, played an important role. The intense pressure they were
under was a key factor in the widespread
appeal of this "camp" sensibility, one of
the growing gay subculture's distinctive
features.

Like an underground stream spouting
aboveground now and then, the gay subculture and homophile movement went
largely unseen by those not privy to it.
But a dramatic confrontation changed
this course, when Allen Ginsberg's
HOWL, a book of poetry with graphic
homosexual imagery, was seized by the

police in 1957. The ensuing censorship battle, in which the prosecutors tried to have Ginsberg's book declared obscene, resulted in a victory for author and publisher. The following year, *One* Magazine won a similar case against the U.S. Postal Service, which allowed all gay publications use of the U.S. Mail. In effect, as Allen Ginsberg claims, the censorship forces acted as publicists for a new sensibility. More people than ever now knew about these publications, and more people than ever wanted to read them. By the end of the decade, paperback books with lesbian and gay themes appeared in relatively large numbers, and took on great significance in the lives of lesbians and gay men: they recognized parts of themselves in the characters and came to New York, Los Angeles and San Francisco, looking for the gay world these books often portrayed.

So, while the Fifties were a time of repressive conformity, they also laid the groundwork for the changing consciousness among gay people— from despair and self-hatred to minority group identification— that would reach fruition only a decade later.

Audre Lorde & Maua Adele Ajanaku

In the 1950's, Audre Lorde and Maua Adele Ajanaku were young, gay, Black and living in New York City. Often juggling multiple identities, their stories provide insights into a time and place that is often neglected in chronicles of gay history, Black history and women's history. The civil rights movement profoundly altered the face of American society, and the lives of these two Black lesbians.

A: I used to go to the bars too often, because they were the only place I went to meet people [lesbians].

M: And going into bars in the Village was going into white women's bars. The bouncers ostensibly were there to keep the johns out, but because I was Black, I was also an undesirable... And I knew that someday this was going to have to be my strength and my power but I also knew that, hey, we're all supposed to be the same.

A: In the Fifties if you were different, you were just as suspicious within the gay community as you were in America. You have to remember that the gay girls (that's what we were called then), were a reflection of what was going on around us... The women I ran with, we knew we were outsiders, we knew we were outside the pale. We lived in the Village, we were dykes, a lot of us were artists. We hated typing; we didn't want straight jobs. And this of course was the Fifties. We were like the gay girls version of the beatniks. And even within that group there were divi-

sions; we divided [ourselves] into the blue jeans and the bermuda shorts set... And then there were those of us who straddled it and wore things like riding pants. A lot of this thing [was] symbolized by dress.

M: It was like a social group: groups of people who spent most of their time together — to the clubs together, to the parties, to the beach. I have to always [clarify between] the bars uptown and the bars downtown. Down here in the Village, if I wanted to go to Bagatelle, Swing Rendezvous, Danny's, The Seven Steps, whatever, the thugs who were on the door decided if I went in or not.

A: But the parties, white women's parties never had food! They had little potato chips and dip; well, Black parties always had food. The parties I went to were given by a group of Black lesbians who were a little older than I was. They had cars, some of them were performers, like in Porgy and Bess; they were professional, or semi-professional, women. They were all Black, except for the women who were going with white girls — they'd bring them along.

A: In the Sixties, my identity as a gay girl became less so, because I was involved in the civil rights movement, and I was married, having kids. My consciousness of myself as a lesbian was there, but at that particular moment, I was involved in living another life... The civil rights movement didn't develop as a conflict for me in terms of being gay. Because in the Fifties, that conflict was already there. Even when I was down in the

an interview

Audre Lorde on location with interviewer Jewelle Gomez.

Village, I was also at college; I was a closet student, I was a closet politico, I was involved in progressive movements, but — it was not cool to be homosexual there. The saying then was it made us vulnerable to the FBI, but really it was homophobia. What you had to present to the world was a front, that was impeccable and perfect according to how they defined it. To take the position that, hey, I'm who I am, I don't want to hide — it was the refusal to hide that became questionable and revolutionary.

M: That's equivalent to when Black Americans said, "no more!" They refused to hide... We said "no good!" And then everybody got the feeling that, whatever their oppression was, "well maybe I don't have to take this either."

A: The Black power and the civil rights movement of the late 50's and early 60's was the prototype of every single liberation movement in this country that we are still dealing with today.

The Tumultuous 60s:

By the early Sixties, homosexuality was discussed publicly by religious, legal and medical experts, and in the pages of such popular magazines as *TIME*, *LIFE* and *LOOK*. Like fish in the aquarium, gay people were photographed in bars and on the streets, displayed for all the world to see. In 1964, *LIFE* featured a special story on the homosexual underground, attempting to explain it to mainstream society. This unprecedented interest by the straight world served to decrease gay people's isolation. Here was their subculture (at least the most photographically recognizable aspects) on newsstands across the country. What was perhaps shocking and repelling to the general public actually gave great hope to homophile activists as well as to isolated gay people in small-town America. They understood that although it was "experts" and not gay people themselves speaking, the silence was at least finally broken.

Barbara Gittings recalls:

One of the major successes of the gay movement in the 1960's was our breakthrough into mainstream publicity...As much publicity as possible, that was the whole idea, to crack that shield of invisibility that had always made it difficult to get our message across.

THE NEW YORK TIMES WESTERN EDITION, FRIDAY, DECEMBER 27, 1963.

rowth of Overt Homosexuality Provokes Wide Concern

ndition Can Be Prevented or Cured, Many Experts Say

By ROBERT C. DOTY
Special to The New York Times

NEW YORK.
city's most sensitive open
–the presence of what is
y the greatest homosex-
ulation in the world and
easing openness—has be-
he subject of growing
of psychiatrists, reli-
aders and the police.

nore than a month, this
has discussed the prob-
homosexuality with city
, physicians, social
s and homosexuals
ves.

l inverts have colonized
reas of the city. The
homosexual community
a lodestar, attracting
from all over the coun-
re than a thousand in-
e arrested here annually
ic misdeeds.

he old idea, assiduously
ted by homosexuals,
nosexuality is an inborn,
e disease, has been ex-
by modern psychiatry,
pinion of many experts.
be both prevented and
hese experts say.

ut of the Shadows

a problem that has
n the shadows, protected
os on open discussion
ve only recently begun
eached.

conflicting viewpoints
e today to overcome the
and promote public dis-
.

first is the organized
ile movement—a minor-
ilitant homosexuals that
y agitating for removal
social and cultural dis-
ions against sexual in-

mental to this aim is
ept that homosexuality
curable, congenital dis-
this is disputed by the
scientific evidence) and
mosexuals should be
by an increasingly
society as just another
.

view is challenged by a
group, the analytical
rists, who advocate
o what it calls a head-
approach to homosexu-

reated, Not Born

have what they con-
be overwhelming evi-
at homosexuals are cre-
nerally by ill-adjusted
–not born.

assert that homosexual-
be cured by sophisti-
alytical and therapeutic
ues.

significantly, the weight
ost recent findings sug-
at public discussion of
ure of those parental
s and attitudes that
foster homosexual de-

eral public on "the problems of the sexual deviant."

Some experts believe the numbers of homosexuals in the city are increasing rapidly. Others contend that, as public attitudes have become more tolerant, the homosexuals have tended to be more overt, less concerned with concealing their deviant conduct.

In any case, identifiable homosexuals—perhaps only half of the total—seem to throng Manhattan's Greenwich Village, the East Side from the upper 40's through the 70's and the West 70's. In a fairly restricted area around Eighth Avenue and 42d Street there congregate those who are universally regarded as the dregs of the invert world—the male prostitutes—the painted, grossly effeminate "queens" and those who prey on them.

In each of the first three areas the homosexuals have their own restaurants and bars—some operated for them under the contemptuous designation of "fag joints" by the organized crime syndicate.

They have their favored clothing suppliers who specialize in the tight slacks, short-cut coats and fastidious furnishings favored by many, but by no means all, male homosexuals.

There is a homosexual jargon, once intelligible only to the initiate, but now part of New York slang. The word "gay" has been appropriated as the adjective for homosexual.

The 'Gay' Life

"Is he gay?" a homosexual might ask another of a mutual acquaintance. They would speak of a "gay bar" or a "gay party" and probably derive secret amusement from innocent employment of the word in its original meaning by "straight"—that is, heterosexual—speakers.

The homosexual has a range of gay periodicals that is a kind of distorted mirror image of the straight publishing world.

Thus, from the Mattachine Society and other serious homophile organizations, the homosexual can get publications offering intellectual discussion of his problems.

Newsstands offer a wide range of magazines and papers designed to appeal to inverted sexual tastes. These include many of the so-called body building publications presenting, under the guise of physical culture, photos of scantily-clad, heavily-muscled men, and others peddling outright homosexual pornography in text and illustration.

In summer, the New York homosexual can find vacation spots frequented by his kind—notably parts of Fire Island, a section of the beach at Jacob Riis Park and many others.

First Deputy Police Commissioner John F. Walsh, who says crime syndicate profits from homosexuals.

Msgr. Robert Gallagher, Catholic youth counselor, who sees the problem as sign of moral breakdown.

the law, which punishes homosexual conduct variously as a crime or a misdemeanor.

Accordingly, it has become a prime objective of the homophile movements to obtain repeal of laws that forbid private homosexual acts between consenting adults, even though these are seldom enforced.

In this, they have the support of psychiatrists and some legal authorities. All, including the homosexuals, agree that enforcement of bans on homosexual conduct constituting a public nuisance or involving minors should be rigorously continued.

In each of the last four years, 1,000 to 1,200 men have been arrested in New York for overt homosexual activity. Most — about two-thirds—were arrested under the disorderly conduct statute for soliciting male partners.

Spokesmen for the Mattachine Society complain bitterly against alleged entrapment of homosexuals by plainclothes policemen sent into homosexual haunts. The homophile groups have won some support from civil rights groups in their campaign to outlaw the uncorroborated testimony of an arresting officer as proof of cases of entrapment for soliciting.

Open to Entrapment

The tendency of homosexuals to be promiscuous and seek pick-ups—a tendency recognized even by the gay writer, Donald Webster Cory, in his book "The Homosexual in America"—makes them particularly vulnerable to police entrapment.

Any sexual contact between persons of the same sex is punishable under the sodomy statute. If the action involves any use of force or threat of force or if one of the participants is a minor, sodomy is a felony. There have been about 250 such arrests annually in recent years, with about two- ... of them coming to indict-

homosexual offenses involving minors—usually young men in their late teens rather than juveniles.

Parental concern over this aspect of the problem probably is excessive, according to most psychiatrists and public officials. In the first place, it is observed, truly psychotic inverts who prey upon pre-adolescent boys are no more common than molesters of girl juveniles.

The Borderline Cases

Secondly, prevailing psychiatric opinion is that a single homosexual encounter would be unlikely to turn a young man toward homosexuality unless a predisposition already existed in the individual.

There is general belief, however, that strict enforcement of the law against seduction of minors is important to protect borderline cases from adult influences that could swing them toward homosexual orientation when heterosexual adjustment was still possible.

Commissioner Walsh, officials of the State Liquor Authority and New York homosexuals agree that there is evidence that the crime syndicate had moved into the operation of bars and night-spots for homosexuals as early as 1957.

The police and the liqour authority have closed, temporarily or permanently, scores of places —more than 30 last year alone —where disorderly conduct involving homosexuals was established.

"There is no direct proof of syndicate operation, but on more than one occasion we have had the same persons employed in this type of place as manager, bartender or doorman, indicating some sort of organization," Commissioner Walsh says.

He acknowledges that this may involve some low-level police pay offs but says it is unorganized on the police side. The Commissioner's confidential unit

Conflicting Points of View Spur Discussion of Inversion

forming a permanent attachment that would give them the sense of social and emotional stability others derive from heterosexual marriage, but few aehieve it.

The absence of any legal ties, plus the basic emotional instability that is inherent in many homosexuals, cause most such homosexuals' partnerships to founder on the jealousies and personality clashes that a heterosexual union would survive.

Hence, most homosexuals are condemned to a life of promiscuity—the cruising of bars seeking casual partners.

It is miscalculation in this almost inevitable phase of their lives that most often brings homosexuals into conflict with the law. This peril, however, is becoming less menacing.

"From homosexual subjects treated 25 years ago we learned that finding a paramour was a difficult and dangerous undertaking," wrote Dr. Abram Kardiner, a leading authority in the field, nine years ago. "Today [1954] we learn they are plentiful, in all walks of life, with no risks involved. They are to be found in bars, restaurants, theaters, public toilets, in the factories and universities."

Inverts are to be found in every conceivable line of work from truck driving to coupon clipping. But they are most concentrated—or most noticeable—in the fields of the creative and performing arts and industries serving women's beauty and fashion needs.

Their presence in creative activity is not, as an old myth fostered by homosexuals would have it, because inverts tend to have superior intellect and talent. Most students of the subject agree that the significant factor in homosexual colonization of some of the arts is that men who would find difficulty in winning acceptance from fellow workers in more prosaic activities naturally gravitate toward solitary, introspective endeavor.

The list of homosexuals in the theater is long, distinguished and international. It is also self-perpetuating.

There is a cliquishness about gay individuals that often leads one who achieves influential position in the theater—as many of them do—to choose for employment another homosexual candidate over a straight applicant, unless the latter had an indisputable edge of talent that would bear on the artistic success of the venture.

Not Immune to Women

There is a popular belief that homosexuals are immune to sexual attraction by women. Dr. Irving Bieber, director of the most recent extensive study of homosexuality, disputes this

Robert Gallagher of the Youth Counseling Service of the Roman Catholic Archdiocese of New York.

"I believe there are some signs of recognition of the nature of this breakdown and of reaction against it. We refuse to let homosexuals say they are irresponsible. We try to help them to exercise human responsibility and give them the encouragement that religion has to offer. Parish priests are advised under our pastoral counseling program to urge homosexuals to seek psychiatric help."

This expressed the general approach of other churchmen consulted.

In a nine-year study—"Homosexuality—a Psychoanalytic Study of Male Homosexuals"—that won international attention last year, Dr. Bieber, associate clinical professor of psychiatry, New York Medical College, and nine associates in the same field published evidence that the roots of homosexuality lay in disturbed early family relationships.

In almost every homosexual case, they found some combination of what they termed a "close-binding, intimate" mother and-or a hostile, detached or unrespected father, or other parental aberrations.

"The father played an essential and determining role in the homosexual outcome of his son," the Bieber group reported flatly. "In the majority of instances the father was explicitly hostile . . .

"We have come to the conclusion [that] a constructive, supportive, warmly related father precludes the possibility of a homosexual son; he acts as a neutralizing, protective agent should the mother make seductive or close-binding attempts."

The group reported that 27 per cent of the homosexuals under treatment by the group achieved a heterosexual orientation.

The organized homosexuals dispute the validity of psychiatric findings on deviants. They argue that the medical students of the problem see only those homosexuals who are disturbed enough to seek treatment. Therefore, they say, findings based on that sample cannot be applied to the majority of "adjusted" homosexuals.

To this, Dr. Bieber replies that, during his wartime service, he interviewed intensively about 75 homosexuals discovered by military authorities. Among these involuntary subjects for study he found no basic differences in their psychopathology from that of the voluntary group under treatment, except that the former were more defensive and re-

HOMOSEXUALITY

A secret world grows open and bolder. Society is forced to look at it—and try to understand it

These brawny young men in their leather caps, shirts, jackets and pants are practicing homosexuals, men who turn to other men for affection and sexual satisfaction. They are part of what they call the "gay world," which is actually a sad and often sordid world. On these pages, LIFE reports on homosexuality in America, on its locale and habits (*pp. 66-74*) and sums up (*pp. 76-80*) what science knows and seeks to know about it.

Homosexuality shears across the spectrum of American life—the professions, the arts, business and labor. It always has. But today, especially in big cities, homosexuals are discarding their furtive ways and openly admitting, even flaunting, their deviation. Homosexuals have their own drinking places, their special assignation streets, even their own organizations. And for every obvious homosexual, there are probably nine nearly impossible to detect. This social disorder, which society tries to suppress, has forced itself into the public eye because it does present a problem—and parents especially are concerned. The myth and misconception with which homosexuality has so long been clothed must be cleared away, not to condone it but to cope with it.

Photographed for LIFE by BILL EPPRIDGE

A San Francisco bar run for and by homosexuals is crowded with patrons who wear leather jackets, make a show of masculinity and scorn effeminate members of their world. Mural shows men in leather.

IN AMERICA

CONTINUED

Gay rights activist Barbara Gittings leads a protest in 1965 calling for federal government hiring of homosexuals.

For those working in the homophile movement and its press, these developments heralded a new age. The gay and lesbian subculture was growing and becoming more self-confident. Social and educational organizations now existed, not only on the coasts but in Midwest cities such as Kansas City, Cleveland and Chicago, providing a network replete with magazines, bars and social outings. The homophile rights movement, still fledgling, patterned itself after the political protest techniques of civil rights leaders. According to poet Audre Lorde,

The Black power and civil rights movement of the late 50's and early 60's was the prototype of every single liberation movement in this country that we are still dealing with.

Gay activists gradually began to believe it was the attitudes of the society around them rather than the behavior of gay people that needed to change. Prior to this, a negative self-image informed by the views of the dominant society had shaped even the thinking of gay activists. As this focus shifted and the self-image of gay people began to improve, a number even participated in picket lines and demonstrations for equal job opportunities and protection from discrimination. The first gay picket line in the United

States was organized by the Homophile League of New York, led by a young activist named Randy Wicker. This was in 1963 at Whitehall Induction Center, where 12 demonstrators protested violations of draft record confidentiality pertaining to homosexuals. The following years witnessed a small yet marked increase in public demonstrations for gay rights, with actions in Los Angeles, New York, Philadelphia and Washington,D.C. Organizers of the homophile movement called them "dignified demonstrations,"

for they, unlike the anti-war, student and Black Power protesters, were not trying to resist — but rather be accepted into — mainstream society.

The psychiatric profession still treated homosexuality as a pathological character disorder, and certainly many gay people continued to buy into this belief. But even the fact that the subject in the mid-1960's was widely debated made it increasingly possible for gay people to refute this stance, and to trust their own feelings, judgement and experiences.

Craig Rodwell opened America's first gay bookstore in the heart of Greenwich Village in 1967. An activist since the 1960's homophile movement, Rodwell sees tremendous change since then:

It's hard for young people today (1982) to imagine that as little as 20 years ago a hundred gay people were sitting around arguing over whether or not they should say that they weren't mentally ill.

Two other influences on the growing homophile movement, and on the growing gay community that did not identify itself as activist, were the appearances in the late 1960's of the women's liberation movement, and the hippies or flower children. As teacher and activist Maua Adele Ajanaku describes,

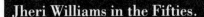

Jheri Williams in the Fifties.

African-Americans said "no more!"
They refused to hide behind the
stereotypes we were supposed to
have. We said "no good! no good!"
And then everybody got to feeling,
whatever their oppression was, "well
maybe I don't have to take this
either!"

The cumulative affect of these movements for social change and ideas of liberation contributed further to the feeling
that gay people too had a choice about
how to live their lives. The political and
social philosophies of the 1960s began to
influence gay men and lesbians profoundly. Clothing designer Jheri Williams says,

The role playing was not as obvious.
It wasn't important...I think one of
the things I realized [in the Sixties]
was, in order for me to be a homosex-
ual it didn't mean that I was woman's
replacement, it didn't mean that I
had to be a "femme." It just meant
that I was a guy who liked guys.

The underground press was born out
of the political protest, rock 'n roll culture resistance, and Black Power movements of the 1960s, and by its height in
1968-1970, there were hundreds of such
newspapers across the country. The

underground press did not embrace openly gay staff members or stories any more than the early women's movement embraced lesbians, but its existence set the stage for the gay movement, and later the lesbian-feminist movement, to create a number of news publications of their own.

The National Organization for Women was founded in 1966, largely by women who were alienated by the subsidiary roles assigned them by men within liberal circles. They wanted equality with men, but they were not radicals calling for a total restructuring of society.

A more radical movement, women's liberation, was founded by women who rejected the male chauvinist posturing found in the New Left, the student, the civil rights, and the anti-war movements. Like gays in the Black civil rights movement, many lesbians remained closeted in the burgeoning women's movement, and for good reason. NOW leaders termed lesbians to be "the lavender menace," again assigning them the role of deviants and sparking a division that was damaging both to the movement and to the individuals involved. Bunny McCulloch, now an ardent feminist and lesbian archivist, says in "Before Stonewall" that she never related to the early women's movement because it was for straight women; since she had never married or cooked for a man, why did she need a movement to free her from "heterosexual bondage?" On the other hand, the movement emphasized that women could have a range of careers and lifestyles, rather than be limited to the socially ordained roles of housewife and mother; for many lesbians this was a long overdue affirmation.

In 1967, *The Ladder* proclaimed that lesbians had more in common with heterosexual women than gay men, which sparked a series of letters and debates within the homophile and the women's movements. It wasn't until after the Stonewall riots in June 1969 that more than a handful of lesbians began to make connections between their oppression as women and as homosexuals, and lesbian-feminism became the vanguard of the women's movement.

As the 1960's progressed, the country was increasingly embroiled in enormous social turmoil. 1968 was a particularly volatile year, full of contradictions and extremes. Martin Luther King, Jr. and Robert Kennedy, liberal leaders of great magnitude, were assassinated. In the aftermath of King's death, riots spread through Black communities in over 100 American cities. Anti-war protests moved from campuses into the general populace, making Vietnam our most unpopular war. The Democratic Party convention, held in Chicago in August of 1968, proved to be a battleground, both on the streets and inside the convention hall. The climate of rage continued into the summer of 1969. Craig Rodwell recalls,

There was a very volatile political feeling, especially among young people. And when the night of the Stonewall riots came along, just everything came together at that one moment. People quite often ask, "What was special about that night, Friday, June 27, 1969?" There was no one thing that was special about it. It was just everything coming together, one of those moments in history where, if you were there, you just knew that this is IT. This is what we've been waiting for.

On this night, gay patrons of the Stonewall Inn spontaneously decided to fight back against the police harassment to which they had long acquiesced. It was time for the small but vocal number of gay activists and the flourishing gay bar culture to join forces and claim their place in the new social landscape. The Stonewall riots signified the end of a long era of fear and intimidation. With the speed of a prairie fire, a highly visible and vital movement for gay and lesbian liberation emerged as an important social and political force.

Donna and Val in the '40s (a photo Donna particularly likes)

Becoming Visible:

On Doing Visual Research in Lesbian & Gay History

by Andrea Weiss

January 1983: I'm at Donna Smith's house in Marina del Rey. We're leafing through an old, worn photo album. Donna is transported back in time, rambling from one story to the next about her 40 years lived with Valerie. Beyond her voice the house seems oddly still. I, too, miss what I imagine was Val's presence, that filled the house for so many years. It's growing late, so I gently interrupt to make sure Donna understands which of her photographs I want her to reproduce. The one of them together, outdoors, by a tree..."Oh, no," Donna responds. "You can't possibly use that... I've always hated that dress on Val. No, you simply cannot have that photo."

April 1983: Every time I go into a film archive and tell them the subject of my research, the response is the same. A moment's pause, then closer scrutiny. Then: "Uh, we don't, I'm sure we don't have any film footage of homosexuals." But today I remain undaunted, and head for the dusty file cabinets. Hours pass, and I've exhausted any likely subject headings: transvestites, cross-dressing, Greenwich Village, sexual perversion, oddities. I'm about to submit to the archivist's greater wisdom, when something pulls me over to the file on police reports. Sure enough, there's footage of a vice squad raid on a New York gay drag bar in 1959. Gay people are everywhere, only hidden from view.

There's an inherent dilemma in trying to uncover the visual artifacts of a largely invisible subculture. As the primary researcher for "Before Stonewall," I found this dilemma manifesting itself daily. I was searching for fragments with which to reconstruct a history, but I was also looking for something different: the visual signs and symbols that suggest an iconography unique to the lesbian and gay community.

What I found are essentially two histories that run parallel, sometimes merging, sometimes contradicting each other: the representation of homosexuality by the dominant culture, and a portrayal of the lesbian and gay subculture as seen through its own eyes. The latter, based on home movies, photo albums, and other memorabilia, can provide a vital foundation for interpreting images that have had a particular meaning (or meanings) to lesbians and gay men, while invisible to the rest of the world.

The mass media, on the other hand, has the tendency to flatten rather than highlight the various textures of anything, and of homosexuality in particular. The absurdly stereotypical images of Hollywood films could, however, be used in "Before Stonewall" in ways that inverted the originally intended meaning. For example, we were able to find an early silent comedy featuring a "sissy" cowboy; to this we added an old, very silly Country/Western tune about a "lavender cowboy," in order to explode the heterosexual myth of the virile, womanizing cowboy who conquered the Old West. In some cases, we were able to collect material that had slight gay or "camp" overtones but primarily served a much different purpose; when put into the context of "Before Stonewall," these overtones became quite pronounced and startling.

It became even more a question of *how* than it was of *where* to look. When I went to the National Archives — and of course received the standard response — I watched a newsreel of soldiers in training during World War II. Thinking back to the "Uh, we, I'm sorry but we don't have any film footage of homosexuals," I wondered, who is to say that these men aren't homosexual? Even by Kinsey's statistics, some are. I would argue that by using this army footage juxtaposed to stories of gay soldiers, and thereby giving the implication of homosexuality, we are not taking images out of context but rather putting them back in.

There's something else about these particular images of soldiers, though. I was especially struck by the careful cinematography, unusual in 1940's newsreels. Since it's safe to assume the film was shot by a man (even today women are rarely behind the camera), the soldiers are presented in a visually exciting and loving way that clearly suggests homoeroticism. But, then again, this material is considered by the archives as standard stock footage. No homosexuals here. The process of unearthing a gay iconography involves seeing with double vision. Absence as image. Erasure as image.

If lesbian and gay people have paid a price for this invisibility, it must be pointed out the terrible price *visibility* has also exacted. One man, whose voice we hear on a 1963 radio program, discusses how he expects to lose his job as a result of this broadcast. Twenty years later, a woman living with this same fear agrees to be interviewed for "Before Stonewall" only if she is backlit so her identity won't be revealed. Past connects with present as her story of being hounded out of the Air Force during the McCarthy era is told over an image of profound absence.

It's important, I think, in a film such as "Before Stonewall," whose existence is in itself a remarkable indication of how much things have changed over the years, to also show how much they have not. What historian and playwright Martin Duberman, interviewed in the film, says of the 1950s is true today as well:

It's not as though the '50s were a time

of complete desperation. It depends
on who you were, where you were,
how lucky you were. We had a group
of supportive friends; there were
some bars you could go to...

Just as Duberman recounts his (relatively) good fortune in the 1950s, the film
cuts to Red Jordan Arobateau, a Black
woman who contradicts the image
Duberman has presented of the comfortable, supportive environment he was able
to find:

The bar scene was just miserable.
And when you say, "Did you find a
bar to go to?," it wasn't that easy at
all back then.

The film takes a one step forward,
two steps back approach; rather than
trying to speak for all gay people and present a uniform or linear picture of what
gay life was like in a particular period, it
offers a range of experiences, varying
with, as Duberman says, who you were,
and how lucky.
We tried, in "Before Stonewall", not
to oversimplify the experiences of lesbians and gay men in order to promote
some neat theory; we didn't want to
"clean up" the image in order to be
accommodating and non-offensive to the
straight, middle-class values of main-

stream culture. One person says in the film, "We thought we could be accepted, by them not knowing who we were." But of course, that's not acceptance at all. "Before Stonewall" rejects the notions of sameness and invisibility, forms of "passing" that will not protect the gay community from the current health crisis or from rising anti-gay violence. Instead the film attempts to restore the visual past of a people who have been historically rendered invisible, to reconstruct a rich and diverse history that can nourish the gay community while having much to teach society as a whole.

Discussion Guide

Preparation for Instructors

It is important that, in teaching about homosexuality, distortions and misrepresentations are not perpetuated.

Therefore, it is highly recommended that teachers read in advance some of the material from the suggested reading list, and prepare themselves to speak knowledgeably and comfortably about the subject. If possible, teachers should preview "Before Stonewall" when the film arrives to be familiar with its style and content. If this is not possible, this guide briefly outlines each section of the film, so that the instructor will be aware of the major themes and topics to be raised. We recommend you summarize the highpoints of the film, so that students have some preparation for the screenings.

Because of the vast amounts of new information presented in each reel, you may want to screen it in 30 minute sections, with discussions following each. It may also be useful to have a guest speaker, either one of the filmmakers or someone from a local gay organization. National organizations are listed at the back of this book and often will assist with recommendations for a speaker in your region. The film invariably raises many questions that the speaker may be in a better position to answer. However, it is not required that all questions be answered; often formulating the questions and thinking about them can in itself be an important learning experience.

Before Viewing the Film

Before the film is shown it might be useful to initiate a discussion with students which will elicit what they already understand about homosexuality and what ideas they hold. This discussion would offer the opportunity to correct gross misconceptions prior to the screening of the film, and permit students to view it from a more open-minded perspective. The students' knowledge might be evaluated by having them define terms such as homosexuality, homophobia, and perhaps discrimination, oppression, and prejudice. After the viewing of the film, any misconceptions that were voiced could be raised again to determine if new understandings have been reached.

The following questions could be raised to your class prior to the screening, so that students can look for and think about answers during the film. Seeking answers to specific questions will help students be more actively attentive during the watching of the film.

1. What is a subculture? A minority group? Do homosexuals constitute a subculture or minority group?

2. What are some of the differences between gay male and lesbian history? What are the possible causes of these differences?

3. Do you think it would be a difficult task to research gay and lesbian history? Why or why not? What would some of the obstacles be?

4. Do you think the situation in the U.S. has changed significantly for lesbians and gay men? In what way? How has it not changed?

After the Film Screening

If a guest speaker has been invited, have this speaker address the class or group after the screening to answer questions raised by the film. Otherwise, review the study questions you posed before the screening. In addition, you might ask students the following:

1. What, according to the film, has been the ideology of our society about homosexuality? How is this ideology translated into the actual

oppression of gay people?

2. How did the various people who appear in the film respond to oppression? Why are some people victims and others resisters, and is it possible to be both at once?

3. What does resistance mean? What forms, overt and covert, could it take? How did the people in the film resist?

In discussing the film, it is often useful to break into small discussion groups in order for students to express their feelings about what they've seen. The small group discussions might begin with emotional responses, and then move on to more substantive questions raised by the film. A designated "leader" could pose several questions for small group discussion, selected from the questions found in this study guide. When the entire class reunites, each group will have something different to contribute to the whole.

Suggestions for Class Assignments

1. Conduct an oral history interview with a relative or friend who lived through some experience of discrimination or oppression. Prepare questions in advance that would elicit both personal experience and a

broader perspective on the era. Tape record the interview. Listen to the tape for what the person reveals about his or her life in a particular time period and the effects of social discrimination or oppression on the individual's life. Share these findings with the class.

2. Read several current popular magazines and analyze them from the perspective of a historian in the future. What do the articles, ads, headlines, pictures and design of the magazines tell you about the time period and culture? The position of women, minorities, homosexuals? What values and priorities are reflected? Not reflected? Share these findings with the class.

3. Keep a journal for several days or a week which records everything you hear or see that relates to either homosexuality or heterosexuality. What everyday aspects of our culture assume that heterosexuality is the norm? How prevalent is this assumption? What, if anything, is mentioned that pertains to a homosexual lifestyle? In what ways do the findings relate to the experiences of the people who speak in "Before Stonewall?" Based on the journal entries, can you assess how things have changed, or not changed?

Suggesed Reading List

Altman, Dennis. *The Homosexualization of America and the Americanization of the Homosexual*. New York: St. Martin's Press, 1982.

Berube, Allan. "Coming Out Under Fire." *Mother Jones*, January 1983.

Cook, Blanche Wiesen. *Women and Support Networks*. New York: Out and Out Books, 1979.

D'Emilio, John. *Sexual Politics, Sexual Communities: the Making of a Homosexual Community in the United States, 1940-1970*. Chicago: Univ. of Chicago Press, 1983.

Duberman, Martin Bauml. *About Time: Exploring the Gay Past*. New York: Gay Presses of New York, 1986.

Dyer, Richard (ed.). *Gays and Film*. New York: Zoetrope, 1984.

Faderman, Lillian. *Surpassing the Love of Men*. New York: William Morrow and Company, Inc., 1981.

Garber, Eric. "Tain't Nobody's Business." *The Advocate*, May 13, 1982.

Grahn, Judy. *Another Mother Tongue: Gay Words, Gay Worlds*. Boston: Beacon Press, 1984.

Hall, Radclyffe. *The Well of Loneliness*. New York: Avon, 1981.

Katz, Jonathan Ned. *Gay American History*. New York: Avon, 1976.

Katz, Jonathan Ned. *Gay/Lesbian Almanac*. New York: Harper and Row, 1983.

Leyland, Winston (ed.). *Gay Sunshine Interviews*. San Francisco: Gay Sunshine Press, 1978.

Lorde, Audre. *Zami: A New Spelling of My Name*. Trumansburg, New York: Crossing Press, 1983.

Marotta, Toby. *The Politics of Homosexuality*. Boston: Houghton Mifflin Co., 1981.

Martin, Del and Phyliss Lyon. *Lesbian/Woman*. New York: Bantam, 1972.

Roberts, J.R. *Black Lesbians: An Annotated Bibliography*. Tallahassee: Naiad Press, 1981.

Root, Jane. *Pictures of Women*. London: Pandora Press, 1984.

Russo, Vito. *The Celluloid Closet: Homosexuality in the Movies*. New York: Harper and Row, 1987.

Steakley, James. *The Homosexual Emancipation Movement in Germany*. Salem, NH: Ayer Co., 1975.

Tobin, Kay and Randy Wicker. *The Gay Crusaders*. Salem, NH: Ayer Co., 1972.

Vining, Donald. *A Gay Diary, 1933-1946*. New York: Pepys Press, 1979.

White, Edmund. *The Beautiful Room is Empty*. New York: Alfred Knopf, 1988.

Who's Who in Before Stonewall

RICHARD BRUCE NUGENT, artist and writer, New York. A participant in the Harlem Renaissance, his short stories appeared in Langston Hughes' *Fire.*

HARRY OTIS, former dancer, Los Angeles. Born in Colorado in the gay '90s, he brings another angle to the Wild West.

DONNA SMITH, retired bookkeeper, Los Angeles.

HARRY HAY, political activist, Los Angeles. Co-founder of America's first gay rights organization, The Mattachine Society.

MABEL HAMPTON, former dancer and domestic worker, New York. A dancer in the Roaring '20s, Mabel "does more bothering with straight people now than I ever did in my life."

TED ROLFS, retired Merchant Marine, San Francisco.

ALLEN GINSBERG, poet, New York.

BARBARA GRIER, publisher, Tallahassee. Former editor, *The Ladder* (1967-1972), and founder of Naiad Press, the largest publisher of lesbian literature.

CHUCK ROWLANDS, stage producer, Los Angeles. A founding member of The Mattachine Society.

GEORGE BUSE, newspaper reporter, former Army Chaplain, Chicago.

HANK VILAS, therapist, Berkeley.

JOHNNIE PHELPS, the WAC who squared off with General Eisenhower.

RICKY STREIKER, bar owner, San Francisco.

JIM KEPNER, gay activist, Los Angeles.

CARROLL DAVIS, entertainer, Los Angeles.

DR. EVELYN HOOKER, psychologist, UCLA, Los Angeles. Her ground-breaking studies of gay men were published in 1957. She was chair of the U.S. government's National Institute of Mental Health Task Force on Homosexuality.

PAUL H. CLARKE, retired official, State Department Office of Security, Washington, D.C.

FRANK KAMENY, former U.S. government scientist, Washington, D.C. First person to legally challenge McCarthy's purge of gay government employees.

RED JORDAN AROBATEAU, writer, Oakland.

MARTIN DUBERMAN, historian and playwright, New York. Authorized biographer of Paul Robeson.

DOROTHY (SMILIE) HILLAIRE, Native American activist, Seattle.

TEDDIE BOUTTE, southern belle, Seattle.

JACKIE CACHERO, bull dyke, Seattle.

AUDRE LORDE, poet and university professor, New York. An activist in the '60s Black civil rights movement.

MARGE SUMMIT, bar owner, Chicago.

LISA BEN, former secretary, Los Angeles.

MAUA ADELE AJANAKU, activist and teacher, New York.

JHERI, clothing designer, San Francisco.

NANCY (BUNNY) McCULLOCH, film editor and lesbian archivist, Los Angeles.

ANN BANNON, university professor and writer, Sacramento. Author of the best-sellers of the '50s and '60s, the *Beebo Brinker* series, about lesbian life in Greenwich Village.

CRAIG RODWELL, founder of *Oscar Wilde*, America's first non-porn gay bookstore, New York.

JOSE SARRIA, The Nightingale of Montgomery Street. His operas at the Black Cat drew people from around the world.

GRANT GALLUP, minister, Chicago.

IVY BOTTINI, former housewife, co-founder of New York NOW.

Resources

Before Stonewall (87 minutes, color) is available for rental or purchase in 16mm and in all video formats through Cinema Guild, 1697 Broadway, New York NY 10019 (212) 246-5522.

The filmmakers and the people who appear in the film are often available for speaking engagements, and may be contacted through Jezebel Productions, P.O. Box 1348, New York, NY 10011

Organizations to contact for additional resources and/or possible speakers include:

Gay Film Today
P.O. Box 20207, New York NY 10029

GLAD (Gay and Lesbian Anti-Defamation League)
99 Hudson Street, 14th floor, New York NY 10013

Gay Task Force, American Library Association
P.O. Box 2383, Philadelphia PA 19103

National Gay and Lesbian Task Force
1517 U Street NW, Washington, DC 20009

National Gay Speakers Bureau
P.O. Box 3575, Los Angeles, CA 90078

Parents and Friends of Lesbians and Gays (P-FLAG)
P.O. Box 553, Lenox Hill Station, New York, NY 10021

For a complete listing of gay and lesbian archives, consult the Directory of the International Association of Lesbian and Gay Archives and Libraries, compiled by Alan V. Miller. (Available through Canadian Gay Archives, P.O. Box 639, Station A, Toronto, Ontario M5W 1GZ, Canada.)

You might also look in the phone book under Gay or Lesbian for organizations that may be useful in recommending local speakers to accompany the film.

Production Staff for *Before Stonewall*

BEFORE STONEWALL:
THE MAKING OF A GAY AND LESBIAN COMMUNITY

Directed by Greta Schiller
Executive Producer: John Scagliotti
Co-Director: Robert Rosenberg
Research Director: Andrea Weiss
Editor: Bill Daughton
Assistant Editor: Peter J. Friedman
Narrator: Rita Mae Brown
Cinematographers: Sandi Sissel, Jan Kraepelin, Cathy Zheutlin
Production Coordinator: Amy Chen
Unit Managers: Katherine Grant-Bourne, Tina Schiller, Amy Kato, Pat Mei
Sound: Lori Seligman, Roy Ramsing, J.T. Tagaki
Additional Camera: Jeff Farber
Assistant Camera: Becky Butler, Deborah Sargeant
Additional Assistant Editors: Jan Stott, Damian Begley
Additional Sound: Peter J. Friedman, Beni Matias, Dean Sargeant
Assistants to the Producers: Anne Alexander, Mindy Cohen, Jeff Lunger, Christina Sunley
West Coast Co-Producer: Howard Petrick
Personal Collections Coordinator: Nancy Miller
Personal Collections Researchers: Jewelle Gomez, Neil Miller, Judy Whitaker
Additional Archival Research: Nan Allendorfer, Claudia Gorbman, Larry Horne
Research Assistants: Zane Blaney, Neil Elliot, Jeff Goodman, Janie Groff, Carroll Oliver, Judith Oney, Paul Sergio, Susan Shoiji, Elizabeth Stevens, Sande Zeig
Principal Historical Consultants: Michelle Cliff, Blanche W. Cook, John D'Emilio
Additional Historical Consultants: Deborah Edel, Bruce Eves, John Hammond, Jim Kepner, Toby Marotta, Joan Nestle, Julia Penelope, Judith Schwartz

85

Archival Research Consultants: Hillary Dann, Erica Gottfried,Vito Russo, Tom Waugh
Head Title Design: Jeff Tennyson
Negative Matcher: Noelle Penraat
Photo Animation: Lauren Helf
Opticals: Cynosure
End Title Design: John Bauman
Still Photography: Jan Blair, Bill Jacobson, Judy Whitaker
Special Projects: Augustines Artery, Diana Autin, David Bank, Michael Bumblebee, Kathy Conkey, Greg DeChirico, David Fischer, Scott Gortikov, David Hill, Andrew Kopkind, Terry Lawler, Paula Liss, Linda Matalon, Jay Merritt, Mark Pasley, Lydia Pilcher, Caryn Rogoff, Steven Schnipper, Susan Smith, Chris Straayer, Jan Stuart, Ian Stulberg, Dan Taplitz, Tom Wilson Weinberg, Joe Windish

Special Thanks To: Don Beavers, Alan Berliner, Jack Campbell, Matt Coles, Quentin Crisp, Emile de Antonio, Adrienne Edwards, Bertha Harris, Colin Higgins, Jim Hormel, Lambda Rising Bookstore, Louis Landerson, Long Island Connection, Jeannette Poillon, Stonewall Tours, Marc Weiss, Edmund White and all the other friends and supporters who helped make this film possible.

Funding provided in part by: Corporation for Public Broadcasting, New York Council for the Humanities, New York Council on the Arts, Media Network, National Community Funds.

A few of the publications of
THE NAIAD PRESS, INC.
P.O. Box 10543 ● Tallahassee, Florida 32302
Phone (904) 539-9322
Mail orders welcome. Please include 15% postage.

BEFORE STONEWALL: THE MAKING OF A GAY AND
LESBIAN COMMUNITY by Andrea Weiss & Greta Schiller.
96 pp., 25 illus.   ISBN 0-941483-20-7 $7.95

WE WALK THE BACK OF THE TIGER by Patricia A. Murphy.
192 pp. Romantic Lesbian novel/beginning women's movement.
                                     ISBN 0-941483-13-4   8.95

SUNDAY'S CHILD by Joyce Bright. 216 pp. Lesbian athletics, at
last the novel about sports.   ISBN 0-941483-12-6   8.95

OSTEN'S BAY by Zenobia N. Vole. 204 pp. Sizzling adventure
romance set on Bonaire.   ISBN 0-941483-15-0   8.95

LESSONS IN MURDER by Claire McNab. 216 pp. 1st in a stylish
mystery series.   ISBN 0-941483-14-2   8.95

YELLOWTHROAT by Penny Hayes. 240 pp. Margarita, bandit,
kidnaps Julia.   ISBN 0-941483-10-X   8.95

SAPPHISTRY: THE BOOK OF LESBIAN SEXUALITY by
Pat Califia. 3d edition, revised. 208 pp.   ISBN 0-941483-24-X   8.95

CHERISHED LOVE by Evelyn Kennedy. 192 pp. Erotic
Lesbian love story.   ISBN 0-941483-08-8   8.95

LAST SEPTEMBER by Helen R. Hull. 208 pp. Six stories & a
glorious novella.   ISBN 0-941483-09-6   8.95

THE SECRET IN THE BIRD by Camarin Grae. 312 pp. Striking,
psychological suspense novel.   ISBN 0-941483-05-3   8.95

TO THE LIGHTNING by Catherine Ennis. 208 pp. Romantic
Lesbian 'Robinson Crusoe' adventure. ISBN 0-941483-06-1   8.95

THE OTHER SIDE OF VENUS by Shirley Verel. 224 pp.
Luminous, romantic love story.   ISBN 0-941483-07-X   8.95

DREAMS AND SWORDS by Katherine V. Forrest. 192 pp.
Romantic, erotic, imaginative stories.   ISBN 0-941483-03-7   8.95

MEMORY BOARD by Jane Rule. 336 pp. Memorable novel
about an aging Lesbian couple.   ISBN 0-941483-02-9   8.95

THE ALWAYS ANONYMOUS BEAST by Lauren Wright
Douglas. 224 pp. A Caitlin Reese mystery. First in a series.
                                     ISBN 0-941483-04-5   8.95

SEARCHING FOR SPRING by Patricia A. Murphy. 224 pp.
Novel about the recovery of love.   ISBN 0-941483-00-2   8.95

DUSTY'S QUEEN OF HEARTS DINER by Lee Lynch. 240 pp.
Romantic blue-collar novel.   ISBN 0-941483-01-0   8.95

PARENTS MATTER by Ann Muller. 240 pp. Parents'
relationships with Lesbian daughters and gay sons.
                                               ISBN 0-930044-91-6   9.95

THE PEARLS by Shelley Smith. 176 pp. Passion and fun in
the Caribbean sun.   ISBN 0-930044-93-2   7.95

MAGDALENA by Sarah Aldridge. 352 pp. Epic Lesbian novel
set on three continents.   ISBN 0-930044-99-1   8.95

THE BLACK AND WHITE OF IT by Ann Allen Shockley.
144 pp. Short stories.   ISBN 0-930044-96-7   7.95

SAY JESUS AND COME TO ME by Ann Allen Shockley. 288
pp. Contemporary romance.   ISBN 0-930044-98-3   8.95

LOVING HER by Ann Allen Shockley. 192 pp. Romantic love
story.   ISBN 0-930044-97-5   7.95

MURDER AT THE NIGHTWOOD BAR by Katherine V.
Forrest. 240 pp. A Kate Delafield mystery. Second in a series.
                                               ISBN 0-930044-92-4   8.95

ZOE'S BOOK by Gail Pass. 224 pp. Passionate, obsessive love
story.   ISBN 0-930044-95-9   7.95

WINGED DANCER by Camarin Grae. 228 pp. Erotic Lesbian
adventure story.   ISBN 0-930044-88-6   8.95

PAZ by Camarin Grae. 336 pp. Romantic Lesbian adventurer
with the power to change the world.   ISBN 0-930044-89-4   8.95

SOUL SNATCHER by Camarin Grae. 224 pp. A puzzle, an
adventure, a mystery — Lesbian romance.   ISBN 0-930044-90-8   8.95

THE LOVE OF GOOD WOMEN by Isabel Miller. 224 pp.
Long-awaited new novel by the author of the beloved *Patience
and Sarah.*   ISBN 0-930044-81-9   8.95

THE HOUSE AT PELHAM FALLS by Brenda Weathers. 240
pp. Suspenseful Lesbian ghost story.   ISBN 0-930044-79-7   7.95

HOME IN YOUR HANDS by Lee Lynch. 240 pp. More stories
from the author of *Old Dyke Tales.*   ISBN 0-930044-80-0   7.95

EACH HAND A MAP by Anita Skeen. 112 pp. Real-life poems
that touch us all.   ISBN 0-930044-82-7   6.95

SURPLUS by Sylvia Stevenson. 342 pp. A classic early Lesbian
novel.   ISBN 0-930044-78-9   6.95

These are just a few of the many Naiad Press titles — we are the oldest and
largest lesbian/feminist publishing company in the world. Please request a
complete catalog. We offer personal service; we encourage and welcome
direct mail orders from individuals who have limited access to bookstores
carrying our publications.